The

ACHING UNREST

of

SPHERES

poems

Clint Frakes

Finishing Line Press
Georgetown, Kentucky

The

ACHING UNREST

of

SPHERES

ACKNOWLEDGMENTS

"A Father's Song for Water" in an Elik Press pamphlet
"Paradise Confession" in *Centrifugal Eye*
"Desire #4" in *Zone* and *Ditch*
 "Dream with Willie Mays" in *Orange Room Review*
"Chelonia Mydas" in *Bamboo Ridge #91* and *Conte*
"Colorado River Poem" in *The Sonoran Review* and *You Are Here*
"Flintstones, The Lost Episodes: #72" in *Ditch* and *Bamboo Ridge*
"Desire #28" in *Zone*
"Mail from Tunis" in *Hawaii Pacific Review* and *The Emily Dickinson Journal*
"Mystery Not Always Unkind" in *Best New Poets of 2008*

Publisher: Leah Huete de Maines
Editor: Christen Kincaid
Cover Art: Clint Frakes
Author Photo: Clint Frakes
Cover Design: Elizabeth Maines McCleavy

Order online: www.finishinglinepress.com
also available on amazon.com

Author inquiries and mail orders:
Finishing Line Press
PO Box 1626
Georgetown, Kentucky 40324
USA

Contents

for Kimberley—

Ever since the gods planted their
  Light-Gardens where our flesh meets,
that majestic shadow has quickened near.

An Old Story

for Dinah Crow Dog

Way down below in the cave of our beginning
there's an old woman in buckskin, cooking corn stew.
Her face is an oak burl & the stars & moon
follow the motion of her stirring stick.
Her shawl sways north to south along the Milky Way,
moving the Four Winds above the earth.
For a hundred thousand years *shunka sapa*
has studied her every move.
The trickster dog keeps the world spinning—
plucks a porcupine quill from the blanket she sews
& hides it under the rug each time
she limps to the fire to stir the pot.
When she finishes the quillwork the world will end.
We all meet this old woman when we die,
before we're allowed to the Happy Hunting Grounds.
She will offer you a ladle of hot corn stew.
At that moment you're supposed to know what to do—
have prepared for it all your life.
Of course you're hungry.
She smiles & the stew smells good.
Friend, throw it over your shoulder!
This is what they say to do.
That old dog needs to eat.

Colorado River Poem
for Andy Hoffmann

Unbroken flexing momentum
of blue-green earthbound
thunder bursting white
upon itself : collisions
caught in sandstone &
gneiss : long-grooven
cosmogonies lodged
in sedgebank parties
of wading heron:
manifold rim-
thrusted tributaries
banging deathly pure
seeking flattest reach
riffling under pagoda buttes
sluiced at each thirsty town—
sometimes a thick ferrous
swath atop bare schist
tangled in tamarisk—
at other bends, a knuckly
palisade at the placid gray
murk under elephant-faced
cliffs : the labyrinths of
Flaming Gorge, Yampa
& Desolation as one—
armed Powell saw it
in crazed insistence
touched to his marrow
by Permian time:
finally spread irretrievably
thin as a neutral sheet
of fleshless spent
silver: a remnant
sip wedged at the
basin of planetary
conclusion—the

drying muck of
  alluvial
    Yuma
     plain.

A Father's Song for Water

for Quanah

I scarcely have the nerve to enter the poem,
let alone the song of someone else—
let alone the emerald secrets of the dreaming jaguar.
I'm urging my son to learn the names of continents,
their nations & the capitals of states—
their twinkling cities & tragic bridges
in places he's never been & likely will never go.
We find ourselves at the dappling creek again,
water crawling up this giant stone slab
on which we spread our dripping bodies.
Water has a route & I'm supposed to be
an expert on this & should tell him:

I do not know where we are or what time it is.

I kissed a woodpecker feather today
without knowing its course, gender or larger design.
To my son I will have to say:
We must love what we cannot understand
& love it more for our inability.
There was a woman I did not understand,
though I studied her prints like precious
Zuni relics of pueblos past.
The edge of this razor needn't be unsweet
as my brother fixes his hanging rope
& rainforests tumble into hamburgers.

Find something to praise, son, & praise it
with your sweetest breath, even if it turns out
that your father ended up a madman,
high-stepping in the impossible Mogollon hills—
struck by lightning in shit-stained pants.
Do not forget the day we picked massive,
leaking blackberries at the bend in the creek,

pushed their sweetness into our mouths—
held the alien polliwogs with tender hands
& let it all simply wash over us in summer
without measurement or assigning wrong.

For two seasons I screamed into a closet full of toys
until my voice fled—invited every standing tree
to scream with me. I waited for her in dreams
at abandoned airports & vine-covered, blue country houses,
at the purple sunset on the beach of Lake Huron
where the world's water had just dripped from her hair.
The Kingfisher's ancient legs stood there.
I sent this new song to the Four Directions,
begging the wind for reasonable counterpoint—
& she did call months later:

I'm sorry, I'm so sorry. For whatever it's worth, I am sorry.

These were the days of masks & ungraceful distance—
the days they sprayed the sky with aluminum
& we didn't know why.
These were the days the earth baked in our hidden anger
& the promised rain rightly refused us.

It matters not what flag you wave, son—
or if it takes you to battle or prayer:
arrive again to the sweetberry glint of glacial water,
the luminous hexagons of hidden crystals,
faithfully apply the song & search
for the word by which you will be known.

Chelonia mydas
(Hawaiian Green Sea Turtle)

1.

As the yolk sacks shrink & the young
        fatten against their shells,
the egg teeth on the hatchling heads
        pierce the leathery cases
    & the newborns are pipped.
This prompts two more days of rest
        before the marathon.
They hang their heads & flippers from cracked shells
        like tenement dwellers
            peeking from windows.

A single thrashing turtle triggers a tremendous
        collective wriggle.
The clutch pulses in spastic bursts
        as the pit gradually collapses.
Those at the top claw the ceiling while
        others undercut walls.
Base-dwellers tamp falling sand
        & the brood elevates.
A hundred hatchlings then await a thermal cue
        to ascend in a final, unified mosh—
           the last time they will behave as a group.
Refracted wavelight aligns them with their course.

If the night is dim, the beach slope guides the flurry
        of seabound reptile buttons.

2.

Plunging at the shallow sheet flow of a spent wave
        the hatchlings are lifted with the crash
    of the next breaker,
        no longer crawling but thrusting,

wing-like on the littoral fringe.
With palimpsest strokes & insistent seaward bearing,
      they bob below the crests,
    sightless in the first frantic, unburrowed moments
      buoyantly timing sea rhythm.
An integral Cretaceous clock
    pulls them out with uncertain yolk stores,
colliding in ouncling naiveté
      with the primal power that ate
    half their natal atoll
        at French Frigate Shoals.

3.

A lost, solitary pelagic stage ensues,
      fueled at first by frenzied impulse to be at sea,
    then passive migration on sargassum rafts
      amid the Pacific Gyre,
    nipping at snails, sponges & worms.

4.

Her carapace spins in the relentless eddies for years.

5.

She suns occasionally on a fortuitous
        bench or rise of beach.
We don't know how long she wanders.
Through olfaction or taste,
    now the size of a dinner plate,
    she identifies the coast of her ancestors
      as an herbivore nipping
    on sea grass shoots,
aloof to her clan from the start.

6.

Some swim 1400 km in flotillas
    to breed at the Shoals,
    revert to carnivores on the way.

Males occasionally try to copulate with other males
    or random flotsam.

Once he seizes a cow with his claw-like tail,
    they float in grappling tandem for hours.

      She will have scars.

7.

At the froth of the waning breakers
    her leaking myopic eyes
  set on a specific stretch of beach.
So much as a struck match at 100 meters
    will send her back to sea.
She arches her head & nuzzles the sand
    for a whiff of her natal grit,
      a premonition.

Four years ago she dropped a clutch on this same slope.

Her lifting forelimbs plow a furrow.
    Rear limbs shove sand for a shallow body pit
      so the real work can begin.
As if swimming she hollows the nest with scooping rear flippers,
    pausing to sniff the substrate again,
      a slow blink & then fills the
        hole with a prolific jet of eggs
        in glossy serum.

They say to pluck one right then & drink the yolk
    will heal just about anything.

I Cannot Be Your Teacher
for Marvin Bell

I read the poets hungrily on Sunday morning,
taste the sycamores they leaned against—
the steel bridges under which they snuck away
as boys to drink warm gin in July.
Yet I cannot hold their arrowheads with mine,
cite their augured words by rote
or cradle the alpine trails of their hearts.
Instead, I creep into the private hallways
of their dreams, hold my wet babies in the air,
as they did theirs on a cool, blue Michigan summer lawn—
then steal their best lines with a subtle nod.
The poet's life is private breath set free,
an odd, lion-faced boulder in parting canyon mist.
It is a blue and red door bearing the shadow of a tree
where we enter the perfect terrain of ignorance,
chanting the names of everyone we've loved.
It is being unable to put down a brother's poem
until you've received its lesson,
smelled the earth clinging to its spade—
then picking it up again for good measure.
Yes, the early juniper morning had many secrets
in the orange arches of branches that remember everything
as I fiddled with the kitchen blinds,
measuring how much light to let in—
knowing I've given improper salutation
to the ancient dawn that insists
on creating me again.

Mail from Tunis
for Emily

Your unacknowledged clay
teeters on a ruddy peninsula & you remain
wren-like with a butterfly caught in your throat.
None will touch you without first
knowing severest hunger or
lean internal difference.
Wednesday: your skirt traversed the Amherst
earth, moth-like & veiled—
a warm miracle
as you interrogated each capsule & calyx,
your mute chestnut bun aimed at
mighty periphery—
sheets of your mind delivering
the edge of a place.
When the mail from Tunis came
with saffron & nutmeg, you commenced
banging spice for cake,
barefoot among incessant folds
of nimblest light
bursting upon the tree
a pail of milk,
a fly's wing flexing.
At 4 pm something shifted—
you ran fast upstairs,
closed the door.
Your volcano came timidly
as words crash upon the eye
& your daily bread of the sky—
with each cloud a horse's head.
The guest leaves the house—
a bead of brandy in the glass
& your door still quiet as infant's breath
until the cunning reds of morning
ignite this ellipse again.

Paradise Confession

Approaching the Methodist Church at 3 a.m.,
steel end of the blade up my sleeve,
I seize another cluster of fat stems,
make three swift diagonal cuts
& slip a plastic bag over their conspicuous heads:
three more flaming beauties to smuggle into my alcove
where I'll dunk them in tap water &
arrange their rooster-headed spectacle
against the dishwater cinderblock of my north wall.
Appetite for their company sends me
stalking the Oahu heights with ready scissors,
seduced into forbidden family groves
by purple-hooded prongs,
orange flags fanned like startled macaw,
pistils & stamens reaching with magnetic urgency.
They are my secret currency
gathering light still in the next uncertain morning
like the regalia of an Aztecan dance
while on a lush hill
a sweaty Filipino gardener shrugs
over more clipped stalks
as I stare at their raw anatomy
leaping from slender canoes,
pulling their legs like night heron
to other islands.

Desire #4
Thanksgiving Night on Kapiolani Boulevard

*"Woman was an idol of belly-magic. She seemed to swell and give birth by
her own law... Man honored but feared her. She was the black maw that had
spat him forth and would devour him anew. Men...invented culture as a defense
against female nature."*
                                        —Camille Paglia

Thanksgiving night with nowhere to go in Honolulu
    & gratitude is elusive as Maverick does the splits
        in a pink felt hat.
Chastity works her lollipop,
        dropping her Catholic skirt—
& then comes Eclipse hugging a beach ball
        painted like the globe.
Her booty shorts say *Total* & she sits on the world
        to adjust a wandering stocking.

What are the chances a Pine Ridge girl
        would emerge on this archipelagic stage
            2400 miles from Turtle Island?
The zealous DJ introduces her with incongruent hype:
        "Come and see Wiiiiii!"

    Wi means woman.
                        Or sun.
        Depends if there's a soft, nasal *n* at the end.

A dream catcher burned to her sacrum
    with the four sacred colors:
        red north of lowest lumbar
            white disappearing south
                at the cleft of coccyx yellow & black along
                the impossible axis
                    of pelvic east/west—
        its promise of the Seventh Generation.

She's surprised for the first time today when I
        greet her in her grandparents' tongue—
            "Toniktuka hwo?"

She stumbles at her spinning pole
        garter drawn almost inelegantly for a bill.
            "Lakota?" she asks, bending toward me.
Her tongue has a silver bolt through it.
She spills buckets of jasmine hair across my face
    cooler than midnight water &
        from under this tent, I remember
            sage prairie, buffalo and *wasna—*
    timpsula & wojapi,
            black chokecherries.

I tuck an Andrew Jackson in the
        ankle strap of her shiny stiletto:
            the biggest Indian killer of all time—
his face long & freakish in the glint
        of rhinestones & strobelight.
But we should sing in sage beds under cottonwood
        & morning star, skinny-dip in the shallow
    limey creeks at Grass Mountain
            lollop in the *Paha Sapa—*
                its primrose elk trails
        on citrine-belted hillsides,
eating raspberries & rosehips,
            passing secrets mouth to mouth,
                belly to belly.

But her belly has a bolt through it too.
        Custer just a tumbleweed in a winter-count there.
        Crazy Horse himself a faint, curious melody.
        Calendars of Jehovah and Zeus wan & forgotten
                amid the roar of the Wind Cave—
the song of all our beginning.

No, the lolloping won't happen,
            but I *am* her favorite at the bar,
       getting twice her shine as the suits
            from whom she plucks bills perfunctorily
& then eases back my way in some esoteric reward
            for a few words brought across the ocean
                 from her native plain
       where I carried the Tree of Life with ninety warriors
            to the Sun Dance grounds,
                 laid red earth
            on the half-moon altar,
believing there was a center to everything.

Penance

for John Edward Dudley (1958-2020)

A distant petty crime has me doing community service
on a quiet, green campground in high alpine Colorado.
In an orange safety vest & hardhat I empty trash barrels of
Colt .45 cans, fetid bacon, pulp novels & abandoned sandals.
On a fir-clustered knoll, Johnny Cash swings his legs
from a cedar picnic table, swigs a grape soda & begins to strike
dissonant Gregorian chords on his weathered Fender.
His frame rocks from the waist, tossing the fringe
of his suede jacket through the cold, thin air—
shoulders contorting, neck jerking sideways.
He catches a spark of private epiphany &
his tempo accelerates into wild cross-rhythms,
staggered downbeats, improbable Hendrix riffs
dotted with deft walk downs—
his pick-hand flashing like a wet, reptilian tail.
The music erupts, barely controlled & he
squeezes his guitar neck skyward
as if reeling in a marlin.
The storm of sound settles like a Ry Cooder fugue,
circling gently back to its own origin.

His body relaxes as I approach,
the last note dissipating.
He is placidly unsurprised, peers through me
as if speaking to the blue crags of the San Juans:
 "We all leave something unfinished, son."
I nod, holding my garbage.
 "Do you know how many aliases I've burned out?"
His eyes are locked on the sky.
I can't speak but pull two Bibles from the trash.
There are dozens in different shapes & languages.
We kneel in the frost to sing *Amazing Grace*.
The melody expands into mantric syllables,
bending the red light of coming dusk.

We build a small fire on a bald patch of earth,
enumerating our sins as we feed dried grass
& twigs to the growing flame.
The smoke spirals up to the forming snow clouds.
  "Johnny," I say,
  "This has happened before & will happen again."
  "Every Sunday," he says,
  "Every Sunday until it's done right."

Dream with Willie Mays

for Steve Marcotte

Muggy Michigan summer nights I took batting practice
in the cool, gray basement under a bare lightbulb &
sweating copper pipes, surrounded by stripped furniture &
dank boxes of forsaken Tonka trucks & Gumby dolls.
I bounced a tennis ball off the naked cement
& thrashed at it for hours with a fractured yellow bat
penciling manifold score sheets: entire leagues,
statistics & rivalries developed over years.
I re-enacted canonical exploits of the diamond
from Cobb to Kaline—even apocryphal leagues
of my own invention from Mexico & Japan.
Treaties between nations were made—
worlds saved where cinderblock & steel beams
held up the house near the red pine lake.

Willie Mays walks down the stairs in uniform
& stands by the light switch at the left field foul pole.
With a smile serene as Vishnu, he asks for the bat,
takes his stance in the box, delineated by dripping condensation.
I bounce my twistiest knuckle-curve off the wall.
It squirrels back like a washcloth in the wind
& he takes the pitch on the outside corner,
leaning in to assess the movement.

"What was it like coming up in the majors,
being so young & black & all?"

I ask, setting into another wind up,
this time bringing the hard stuff.
He swings late & misses, inspects the duct tape on the bat.
The ball skitters to a stop by the rock salt bags
& corner sump pit. If it had fallen in,
his at bat would have ended by house rules.
He is beyond all conversation of this world—

an omniscient apparition.

I grab at anything more to ask, retrieve the ball,
realizing that if I strike him out
it will send him back beyond the cosmic veil.
Stupid questions leap from my mouth:

*"Have you ever fallen for the buzzer-in-the-hand
handshake trick, or the squirt-in-the-eye carnation trick?
Have you ever mistaken a small cloud for a galaxy?"*

Flintstones: the Lost Episodes
(#72: In Hell)

The stoneroller Flintstone-mobile descends through treacherous Chinese corridors as I watch from a plush, red theater chair. Wilma & Betty are in the back, Fred driving as always, Barney at his side—all with hands on laps, blinking, unaware they are plummeting deeper into a raging inferno. Cartoon-skinned, black-eyed & oblivious, they roll into Hell Café, feuding: Wilma jealous of Betty, Betty lusting Fred, Fred wrathful at Barney—who is witless in his plain brown skins. They ape a bleak existential drama, unaware of their mortal sins, ignorance & aggression—trapped in Jurassic karma. I watch, no longer a spectator at a theater, but with them in the stone café, pretending to read the *Bhagavad-Gita. And Betty!* I'm digging her & she's the only one to notice me, as I'm a semi-etheric being in their reality. She is the chance of salvation for the lot of them. A generic bartender with criss-cross stitching at his neck, a few strands of hair, blinking black eyes & blue tunic observes them from the end of a long, limey corridor: the accountant of akashic slate ledgers. *Am I their angel brought here to minister their sad delivery to Hell?* I order a muffin, brooding at my dolomite table—knowing I'm already too involved with Betty, though she's only an inken image—her spirit fastened & multiplied in my imagination from countless pajama cereal box Saturdays. Fred, forever orange-clad & angry shouts at the root of my cortex. Barney, the suffering doofus stumbling at the quarry, confounded by the slightest complexity of cause & effect—who had the nerve to beget him—even on a sketch pad? Wilma: forsaken & jealous, German-like in her ironed, white apron. I am clueless how to angel them & quote randomly from the sacred text: poorly translated maxims from a blue, chariot-riding Krishna:

> *"I tell you all the soul is uncleaveable, unburnable;*
> *nor can it be wetted or dried—eternal, all-pervading*
> *& immovable is he from everlasting time."*

A reptilian cockatiel squawks the final dark hour from the cold wall. They are fit to be consumed in their own impossible religion, returned to the bardo ink well & source-pond of all image, absolved of every fraud and pretense in the paleo buddha-fields of child memory.

Blood Song #8

for MLP

On a January Road in Maine, you carved
a message of our love in a blanket of ice—
but the photo you took didn't show
the words so faithfully etched.
From across the country
I knew they were there,
content with your tender face in the telling.
There is no hiding a song so sheer
as one human night of foolish bodies
locked in nectar-search.
We may have bent a word or two
to make a point, defended old wounds
as dusk turned to honey—
honey turned to blood
& our blood begged the Sonoran
moon's silver approach.
Little did I know I would one day dig
post-holes in the rain to keep
your mares from wandering.

Desire #28
a Manoa Valentine

Dear Sonya, it's 1:51 a.m. & I'm drunk,
rebuking the ruse of St. Valentine,
glued to yellowing Taoist lines
on a balmy night, like a raft on the Yangtze—
bristling calm, eying the opulent shore.
It isn't easy to meet Orion's gaze—
his bullets & arrows sheening over my tininess.
Then a final sip of whiskey on the koa stump,
thinking of old chums I thought would never forsake me.
I turn the pages of Tu Fu & find a lottery ticket
my long-gone wife played in '93—
marking the amber scent of a jade mountain song.
Wabi-sabi floods the evening & I hope she probed
the *Arizona Republic* for her lucky numbers,
expected a miracle one autumn,
even if our egg was fried.

No patience for entropy these days,
nor joy in the curve of the moon—
on this, Edgar Poe's birthday!
Nouns gang up on me at Foodland
among the walking dead (now 3 a.m.)
the machinery of lips & Whitmanic glances,
studying varieties of relish.
I think of your Betty Page bangs & how you made
cigarettes taste like chocolate
the night I slid into second base
on the abandoned diamond by Anna Banana's—
certain I'd never do this again & knowing
one usually must be sick before one is brave.
The palms bow softly & for good reason.

What the Poem Should Have Done
for Mehrhoff

It should not have come from a desk,
but a kiosk or black obelisk—
the girth of an oily bridge.
You should find & lose brothers there
in a rainforest or cliff edge.
It should have melted the seam between the
serpents & altars of winter dreams
& the loveless color of alkaline wind.
It should have gained the wealth of rain
with no one watching, held the shape
of what a heart can't imagine—
taller than its words.
It should have been aisles of shiny Nebraska tools
or workboots stuffed with rags.
It should have been broad grass
silently rising in tenement yards
& all that you've loved can fit in it.
It should have been the inexhaustible Tree
with politics of pre-dawn and smoke.
It should have been the uncommon hawk
whose shape disappears in the shoulders
of the West Mountain.

Mystery Not Always Unkind

And who am I? the man sleeping at the border asks, that in my love dream
sleep I have become the guardian of the lion?
    —*Robert Duncan*

John Berryman, where *did* you put those translations?
It's already November & I've conjured 23 oceans in my search.
I looked first under that black Minneapolis bridge,
        then wide Nebraska & its tiled stations,
                murals of gone bison
                        & righteous soft red wheat—
    Oklahoma draped purple in July, like the time
            the cop let me and the yoga girl off with a warning
                    & we ambushed the Super 8 swimming pool
            unbathed & thirsty.
Wyoming was to me just a blown PCV on hot prairie
            & we picked sage until the cavalry came,
                        patient in our dark skin.

Farewell then and now to land speculations.
They say you cannot tear a cloud in half,
            only stare it down until one of you breaks.
After I licked my lips in the crosswinds
            it was half a yellow moon that dried me,
        fresh out of the pool
                under the aching unrest of spheres.

I am not King of the Dead,
            but rising in the ranks
                    eons behind those Jains brushing the earth
            with sapling brooms
                    not to accrue the assassin's weight
                        in a step.

Something beautiful always emerges from underfoot:
            the smell of wet volcanic soil,

                    lean yarrow;
           hummingbirds push on honeysuckle—
                    & even in Detroit
               hawks dive,
                    just like you,

John Berryman,
I can love what I can't understand, but
           it takes an ounce of grace & seasons more kind.
Let's dance then & now
               even if we are poorer than we are sad
                    with fathers fallen under the plow
               & the old Appaloosa curling its lip,
                    brought kicking to the final field.

Clint Frakes is a poet, writer, teacher and naturalist living in Sedona, AZ with his sons, Quanah and Dawson. He was named one of the 50 Best New Poets of 2008 by former Poet Laureate, Mark Strand, and is the former Chief Editor of *The Hawaii Review* and *Big Rain*. He is a graduate of the Naropa Institute Writing and Poetics program (1989) and received his M.A. with emphasis in Creative Writing from Northern Arizona University in 1994. He received his Ph.D. with emphasis in Creative Writing from the University of Hawaii in 2005.